pocket posh® wine

Paulo Carminati

**Andrews McMeel
Publishing, LLC**
Kansas City • Sydney • London

Produced by

DOWNTOWN BOOKWORKS INC.

President Julie Merberg
Senior Vice President Patty Brown
Layout by Laura Smyth/Smythtype Design
Special Thanks Sarah Parvis, LeeAnn Pemberton

POCKET POSH® WINE

copyright © 2011 by Downtown Bookworks, Inc. All rights reserved. Printed in China. No part of this book may be used or reproduced in any manner whatsoever without written permission except in the case of reprints in the context of reviews.

Andrews McMeel Publishing, LLC
an Andrews McMeel Universal company
1130 Walnut Street, Kansas City, Missouri 64106

www.andrewsmcmeel.com

11 12 13 14 15 SHZ 10 9 8 7 6 5 4 3 2 1

ISBN: 978-1-4494-0771-1

Library of Congress Control Number: 2011925220

ATTENTION: SCHOOLS AND BUSINESSES
Andrews McMeel books are available at quantity discounts with bulk purchase for educational, business, or sales promotional use. For information, please e-mail the Andrews McMeel Publishing Special Sales Department:
specialsales@amuniversal.com

contents

introduction vii

translating "winespeak" 1

how to taste wine 15

buying wine 33

memorizing a wine you tried 51

storing wine 57

food and wine pairings 63

organic, biodynamic, and sulfite-free crazes 71

so you want to throw a wine party 85

introduction

Recently, I took a trip with my mother to her childhood home of Pico, part of the Azores Islands archipelago in the middle of the Atlantic Ocean. The last time I visited, I was eleven years old, when the novelty of a new culture and family history couldn't compete with my preteen, pop-culture-obsessed view of the world. I spent most of that trip throwing rocks at lizards scrambling in and out of volcanic rock walls, stopping only to toss the occasional complaint toward my mother. I was too busy pining for a Big Mac to savor and appreciate the farm-fresh meals right in front of me—the killing of chickens and such for the next day's meal, a revolting antiquity compared to the clean, prepackaged, and modern reliability of the supermarket back home. Lastly, and innocently enough, my youth precluded me from indulging in each family's true hallmark: their homemade wine.

Growing up outside Boston in a close-knit community of Portuguese immigrants, I still remember all the nondescript two- and four-liter bottles in the garage, full of homemade wine from this family and that. My father, a Brazilian with Italian roots, gave winemaking a shot but ultimately decided to leave it to our Portuguese friends, to whom winemaking was more than just a hobby. From across the dinner table I would get the occasional telltale whiff: a combination of Concord

wine

grape juice and the breath of that rosy-cheeked guy who sat with his family in the back pews of church every Sunday. Out of curiosity I would ask who made the wine. Whether it was Senhor Calisto, Miguel Pombeiro, or our fourth cousins from Rhode Island, the wine always looked and smelled the same. Amusing, I thought, considering the impassioned descriptions and prideful smiles from the winemakers whenever they gave my parents a few bottles.

The best parts of Pico haven't changed since my last visit. All the meals are still farm fresh, the chickens are killed and the fish are caught hours before a meal, and the gardens overflow with kale and other vegetables. This time, I relished every last bit: the morning breeze off the ocean and the smell of wild mint and dill in the fields. I saw bunches of kale, much better than the expensive organic stuff I buy at home, tossed out for the chickens to eat. From the soup stocks to the fresh eggs to the grass-fed beef, the food was simply better than what I have at home. Everything, that is, except the wine.

At the airport, a simple kiosk explains to tourists Pico's rich winemaking history, complete with all the buzzwords you'd find in Napa Valley or Tuscany. Old Vines. Award-winning. Small production. I've been in the wine industry for years, traveled to wineries and vineyards all over the world, and know what those terms really mean. A combination of wine education, experience, and Generation-X cynicism quickly labeled the kiosk as a marketing tool of the local government meant to bring more travelers and their dollars to the island. This definitely wasn't the Pico I remembered as a child.

Introduction

Yet I remembered all those impassioned, proud, and, most important, authentic wine exchanges from my youth and knew the kiosk really embodied something more true and honest than the average tourist was likely to pick up in the wine.

The main grapes grown on Pico are Isabel and Seibel, two grapes you probably haven't heard of and will never try except for some farmstand wines in the northeastern United States. The grapes are similar to Concord grapes in their bluish-black color, high sugar content, and simple, straightforward flavor. The red wine from these grapes, coincidentally, actually tastes like grapes rather than all the other complex combinations one might get from more "noble" grapes such as Cabernet Sauvignon. The lack of tannins or acidity, combined with the lower alcohol, means the wine has a short life span. The grapes are, for lack of a better term, poor in quality, resulting in an equally "poor" wine. So why, then, does seemingly every family on the island still go through the hassle of maintaining their own vineyards and making their own wine?

The answer seems pretty clear. Why do most of us still make Thanksgiving dinner at home? Surely we could go to a restaurant where professional chefs could provide us with better food without much difference in cost. The answer lies in the intangibles of the meal: Along with the flavors and quality of ingredients, you also take in the familiar and comfortable surroundings, the expectation and anticipation of the meal, and, most important, the effort expended by people you care about slaving away in the kitchen for hours. All these intangibles make the Thanksgiving meal undeniably better in

wine

exactly the same way the wine in Pico is better to me. Because of my sensitivity to the intangibles (such as the pride beaming from the family friend who made the wine), I appreciated every glass I had in Pico, despite the wine itself. Sure, I would analyze the first couple of tastes out of habit, each time confirming what I expected—sugar to acidity out of balance, lack of structure and finish, and so on—but I loved it anyway.

People buy wine guides specifically for the tangibles. In our spreadsheet-driven society, information is calculated, quantified, and spoon-fed back to us. Wine is no different: The popularity of publications with wine scores telling us which wines we will like confirms this passive approach. To some degree, tangibles will be provided and opinions posited here as well. However, it is the intangibles that make a wine great, and you cannot have intangibles without *tangibles* to juxtapose. True appreciation of wine lies in the back and forth between the two.

So continue to learn as many hard facts as possible. The more you know about regions, grapes, styles, and pairings, the more solid your foundation of tangibles will be. Consume as much information as you like, and take advantage of all the outlets available. But with every wine, every time, don't forget to drop your lists and your scores and take a running leap off into the soul of the wine. If you don't find anything, get back up on your foundations and jump off again. What you are ultimately looking for is a special connection between you and that wine, a bond no wine guide or expert can pinpoint.

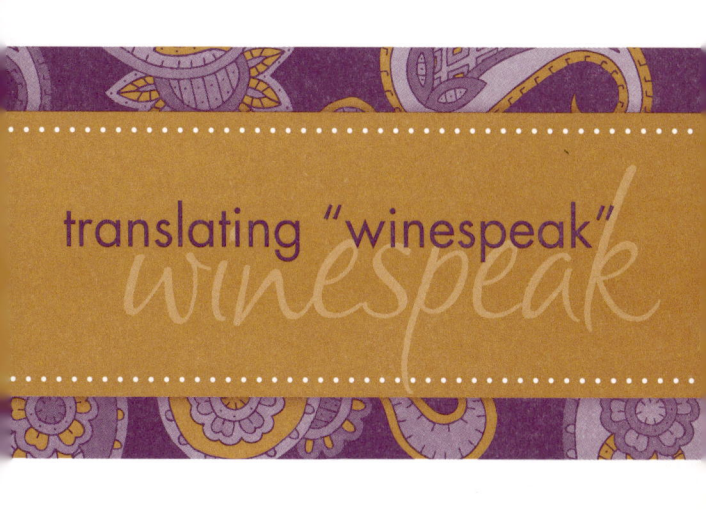

translating "winespeak"

translating "winespeak"

One of the reasons becoming knowledgeable about wine can be so offputting is that those who do know a lot about wine toss out words unfamiliar to most people. Here we try to address some of the more egregious examples of winespeak into terms everyone can understand.

A Winemaking Primer
A lot of winespeak refers to the winemaking process, so let's begin with a quick description of how wine is made, inserting vocabulary explanations where appropriate:

Step One: The grapes grow over the course of a few months. They develop a particular sugar level (known as brix) and acidity.

Step Two: When the grapes are ripe, they are harvested and either pressed to extract the juice (most white wines) or crushed into a combination of skins and juice called the must (most red wines). Yeast is added and feeds off of the sugars, resulting in carbon dioxide (which escapes into the atmosphere) and alcohol (which gives the wine structure and body).

wine

Step Three: A secondary fermentation may sometimes occur that converts the natural malic acid of grapes (think apples) to lactic acid (think dairy products).

Step Four: The wine can then be aged or bottled directly.

Winespeak

Aperitif: This means the wine is good as an appetizer. Usually light, crisp, and consumed on their own or with lighter fare, these wines are meant to cleanse and prep the palate for what's to come. Sparkling wine, Sauvignon Blanc, and dry, crisp rosés fall into this category.

Appellation: A geographically delineated wine region, recognized by the appropriate governing bodies in each country. For example, France has its A.O.C. (Appellation d'Origine Contrôlée), and Italy has its D.O.C. (Denominazione di Origine Controllata). This way, there's no mistaking whether a wine comes from Napa, for example, or just outside.

Aroma: The three levels of aromas in wine come from the three stages of a wine's life. Primary aromas are derived from the grape itself (fruits and woody stems), secondary aromas from the winemaking process, and tertiary aromas from the wine as it ages. The aromas from barrel aging straddle both secondary and tertiary, but bottle aging is always tertiary.

Translating "Winespeak"

Barrels (*barriques* in French): Usually made of oak and used to age wine. The oak is semipermeable, allowing for a very slow, steady exposure to air and a controlled environment for wine to develop and age accordingly. Malolactic fermentation commonly occurs in oak barrels. See *Malolactic fermentation*.

Blind tasting: When people try and assess a wine without knowing anything about it. Meant to showcase a person's talent in tasting wine and allow one to evaluate the wine without any preconceptions (such as those based on the price or producer).

Bodega: Wine cellar in Spanish (*adega* in Portuguese, *cantina* in Italian). For cultures where many families make their own wine for consumption, *bodega* also implies a family's summer house or cottage (where the wine is usually made and stored).

Bordeaux: A region in southwestern France famous for its Cabernet Sauvignon–based and Merlot-based red wines. Traditionally a "Bordeaux" blend consisted of five grapes: Cabernet Sauvignon, Merlot, Cabernet Franc, Petit Verdot, and Malbec.

Bouquet: Either the combination of a wine's aromas or another way of saying a wine's tertiary aroma, depending on whom you ask. Sometimes defined as human-made (i.e., the winemaker's influence) scents rather than those intrinsic to the grape.

wine

Breathing: Specifically, letting a wine "breathe." When wine interacts with air, the oxygen breaks down molecules in the wine, releasing more aromas and mellowing out more astringent wines (by oxidizing tannins). Young wines will show more balance and older wines will be reinvigorated, though by how much depends on the wine. See *Decanting*.

Burgundy: A region in eastern France famous for its Pinot Noir (red Burgundy) and Chardonnay (white Burgundy).

Capsule: The top of the wine bottle (usually foil or plastic for screwtops). Meant to seal the cork in and provide identification (when resting in a wine rack).

Carbonic maceration: A fermentation process popular in France's Beaujolais region, where whole grapes are loaded into a sealed vat pumped full of carbon dioxide. The juice from the grapes ferments inside the grape (rather than outside after the grape is pressed). The result is a very fruity wine with hardly any tannins and a hint of bubblegum flavor.

Cépage: French term usually referring to the blend of different grapes in a wine.

Translating "Winespeak"

Chaptalization: When a winemaker adds sugar to the grape must before fermentation. Usually done to compensate for poor grapes with low sugar levels to reach an acceptable alcohol level after fermentation. Illegal in some countries.

Château: Traditional French term for *winery*, originating in Bordeaux.

Claret: A British name for red blends from Bordeaux and similar styles, predominantly Cabernet Sauvignon and Merlot. American clarets are sometimes called Meritage.

Côtes du Rhône: An officially designated French region (A.O.C.) with wines usually featuring the typical blend of red grapes (Grenache, Syrah, and Mourvèdre) from the region.

Cru: French term meaning "growth" and referring to the vines in a particular region. For example, in Burgundy the term *Premier Cru* refers to a "first in class" location of vines and *Grand Cru* a "greatest and in a class of its own" location.

Cult wines: Small production, high-quality, and even higher-demand wines that most people never see or try.

Cuvée: French term, literally meaning "vat" and implying a blend of grapes or wines mixed in said vat.

wine

Decanting: The process of removing the wine from a bottle into another container (e.g., glass, decanter). The purpose is twofold: to remove any sediment that is present in the wine and to aerate the wine.

Dessert wine or digestif: Usually a wine whose higher sugar level and lower acidity are perfect after a meal. Whereas an aperitif causes the mouth to salivate in preparation for more, a digestif has the opposite effect, satisfying the palate after a few sips. Late-harvest wines such as certain Rieslings, eisweins, sauternes, and port wines are some examples.

Eiswein (*ice wine* in English): A dessert wine made from grapes left on the vine so late into the season that the cold weather freezes the water inside the grape. Everything else, including the sugars, remains unfrozen, so the resulting pressing of the grapes produces a very thick, concentrated, and sweet juice.

Estate: Refers to the actual property and winery. *Estate-grown* means the grapes came from the property's own vineyards. *Estate-bottled* can mean the wine was made and bottled at the winery, but the grapes may have been purchased from someone or somewhere else.

TRANSLATING "WINESPEAK"

Fortified wine: A wine to which alcohol (usually a colorless, flavorless form of brandy) has been added, killing the yeast and halting fermentation. The remaining wine will have a higher sugar content and therefore be much sweeter. Port wine, sherry, and Madeira are all fortified wines.

Malolactic fermentation: The process whereby a bacteria convert malic acid (think tart green apples) to lactic acid (round and buttery, as in yogurt). Although it occurs in all red wines, the winemaker can choose to what degree white wines undergo malolactic fermentation, depending on the style of wine desired.

Mouthfeel: Literally the way a wine reacts to the different receptors in our mouths, from first sip to after the swallow. The common notion of taste is a combination of aromas and mouthfeel.

Négociant: French for "wine trader or merchant." These middlemen do everything from buying grapes from different families and making the wine themselves to merely labeling and selling premade wines. Popular in Burgundy.

New World: Any wine made outside Europe. Stylistically, these wines feature more fruit and less terroir than their Old World counterparts.

wine

Noble rot: A fungus caused by Botrytis that attacks ripe, moist grapes (therefore late in the ripening season). The Botrytis dries out the grape, producing a sweet, concentrated juice when pressed (just like eiswein). This rot shouldn't be confused with gray rot, which is the everyday rot or mold we expect on old fruit in humid conditions. The finest and most expensive Sauternes and German dessert wines all benefit from this "noble" form of Botrytis.

Oeno: A prefix derived from the Greek word *oinos*, or "wine," and pronounced "ee-no." The terms *oenophile* (wine aficionado) and oenology (the study of wine) are the most common examples.

Old World: A wine made in the traditional regions of Europe. These wines tend to feature more terroir and less fruit than New World wines.

Plonk: A British term for cheap wine. Originally plonk also meant poorly made, but the term has been reappropriated to mean "unpretentious and endearing in its affordability."

Punt: The dimple or indent on the bottom of a wine bottle.

Quaff: To enjoy wine without putting much effort or stock in evaluating.

TRANSLATING "WINESPEAK"

Reserve: Usually given to a wine of higher quality, though not necessarily or officially so.

Sommelier: A wine expert knowledgeable in all facets of wine and its storage and service, with restaurants the primary focus. Although an official certification process exists, many sommeliers are "unofficial." A sommelier is always a wine expert, but a wine expert is not necessarily a sommelier unless he or she has been involved in the restaurant and service industry.

Sparkling wine: A wine where the carbon dioxide from the fermentation process has developed into an effervescence rather than escaping into the atmosphere. Sparkling wine can be made anywhere, whereas champagne is made only in the designated appellation of Champagne in France.

Super Tuscan: A style of wine from Tuscany, Italy, whereby a wine was blended with a grape not officially allowed by the controlling body (in this case the D.O.C.). Wines without the D.O.C. certification were usually poor and simple, but certain winemakers in Tuscany knew the quality of the resulting wine would outweigh the lack of D.O.C. certification. Today Super Tuscans are considered some of the best wines from the region.

wine

Tastevin: A silver tasting dish whose shiny, multifaceted surfaced allowed winemakers and sommeliers to discern the quality of wine in dim locations (such as wine cellars). Nowadays some sommeliers still wear them around their necks as a tradition.

Tasting flight: A wine tasting of at least three different wines sampled in the same sitting. Usually about 2 ounces of each wine, intended to be compared with one another.

Terroir: A French term combining the effects of climate, topography, soil, and the manner in which wine from a particular region embodies those unique characteristics. In certain regions rich with winemaking history, winemakers strive for the truest expression of terroir in their wines above all else.

Varietal: Type of grape, as in "My favorite varietal is Cabernet Sauvignon."

Vertical wine tasting: A tasting of multiple vintages of wine, usually of the same wine.

TRANSLATING "WINESPEAK"

Vieilles vignes: "Old vines" in French. Much like the term Reserve, much used and rarely regulated.

Vintage: The designated growing season, harvest, and making of wine within one year. A vintage refers not only to the weather in a given growing season but sometimes to how the vineyard managers and winemakers were able to cope and adjust accordingly. Talented, experienced wineries can still make good wines in "bad" vintages.

Yield: A measurement of the amount of grapes grown. Can be per vine, vineyard, or vintage. Usually the lower the yield, the better the grape quality.

how to taste wine
taste

how to taste wine

Open up most wine guides and you'll find a comprehensive, step-by-step guide to tasting wine, with clear-cut directions and sequences that have all the charm of computer troubleshooting. This approach may be perfect for those who like to assemble furniture or install electronics, but unfortunately many of us are just not wired that way, especially when something as natural as tasting is involved. Tasting wine requires a transition from passive tasting to active tasting, which in turn requires a better understanding of our tasting habits and proclivities.

Thanks to evolution, our first experience with taste is a positive one. Mother's milk or baby formula is the best, most exciting taste we've ever experienced, but only because it's the only one we know. The next step in the development of our palate comes with the introduction of solid foods. Here, for the first time, a "flavor antagonist" is introduced, testing the true function of our sense of taste:

Option 1: Yes, I like this and will continue to eat it.

Option 2: No, I don't like this and will spit it out every time.

wine

Thanks to evolution, this development is as far as it goes for most animals, where whatever tastes good will help them survive and whatever tastes bad will kill them. We're still taking everything on a case-by-case basis as babies, which is why we try to eat everything. Only after a few months do we start associating words, colors, and (later) smells that correspond to those Yes or No flavors, but all those associations do is streamline the process of getting those Yes flavors in our mouths. We hear or see a Yes flavor association, and we will let whoever is around know we want it. Should some association with a No flavor come up, we begin to cry in hopes that we can avoid the No flavor altogether. Eventually our minds begin to categorize those associations further, and when we can finally voice those associations (by talking or pointing) the process of taste becomes as efficient as we need.

By adulthood we've tried hundreds of different foods and sampled thousands of different flavors, but just how different has the process become? We still ask for what we like to eat and refuse what we don't. Years of information and associations help us decide what to eat and drink, to the point that we rarely make a mistake and put a No flavor in our mouths anymore. For all our development over the years, the basic goal of our sense of taste hasn't really changed since we were toddlers. Perhaps now we can pick up different spices in different dishes when we couldn't before or pick up varying levels of salt or sugar, but all that means is that we have more information to call on to help us eat what we want and avoid what we don't.

HOW TO TASTE WINE

So what does all this have to do with tasting wine? For argument's sake, let's say you really like bacon and really don't like brussels sprouts. Could you actually tell a friend why bacon tastes good? Could you describe why brussels sprouts taste bad? Sure, you could cite scientific explanations of dopamine release and all the physiological responses, but most people have a hard time describing why they like the taste of something because they rarely need to do so.

Wine tasting can be frustrating because the old tricks we've been using since childhood to identify flavors often let us down. When most people try a wine they like, they immediately go into association mode, either furiously jotting down as much information as possible or sitting and staring down the label trying to commit it to memory. That approach has worked for almost everything else, but unlike bacon or brussels sprouts, the sheer variety and expanse of taste possibilities connected to wine is too difficult to label with a few simple associations to have within easy reach (unless wine is a No flavor for you, which at this point in the book is doubtful).

As mentioned earlier, the actual process of tasting wine must transition from a passive activity, where your associations have predetermined your reaction, to active tasting, where you determine your reaction on the spot. Active tasting doesn't mean you ignore your associations; rather, that you actually use as many of them as possible to create a new association.

wine

For example, let's say you're traveling and someone brings out a dessert you've never seen or heard of before. You quickly scan it for signs of familiarity: Honey? Check. Peaches? Check. Each time you catch something you recognize, your mind is calculating how much you expect to like it. More often than not, all that work is done before you even try it. Is it visually unrecognizable? Then we immediately go to scent, where maybe we still pick up a faint hint of some fruit (though we can't immediately identify which one). We usually cycle through our nontaste senses, looking for associations, until we finally decide whether we should taste or not.

This brings us to the key fact of wine tasting. Unlike with most things we taste, where our associations lead us to an expected flavor, when we are tasting wine the flavors and scents should lead us to our associations. Surprisingly enough, taste can be just as good a trigger as any other memory, but for some reason to lead with it seems almost backward after decades of doing otherwise. With this understanding, you can learn to lead with the senses and let them guide you to different associations. The real magic about wine tasting is that the associations your senses lead you to aren't limited to just flavors but could be a fantastic trip you took to Europe, or a memorable dinner you had with friends, or countless other moments in your life.

Whether you're trying expensive wine in expensive wine glasses or the two-for-$10 special out of a Dixie cup, the process will be remarkably similar. Unfortunately, most guides to tasting wine are slimmed-down versions of blind-tasting

HOW TO TASTE WINE

guides most sommeliers and industry professionals follow. Wine is essentially a combination of acid, sugar (or fruit), tannin, alcohol, and a bunch of naturally occurring chemical compounds that give wine its flavors. Your sense of smell will pick up all the flavors, and your sense of taste will analyze the rest. Therefore, to avoid the incorrectly coined notion of "tasting the flavors," wine tasters usually discuss the aromas and mouthfeel of a wine. Whatever you'd like to call it, the process of tasting wine is truly special and natural, once you take a few easy steps to help it along.

The Glass
The Riedel Vinum series stemware, a solid standby in the wine world, makes at least fifteen different glasses for different wines. If you have some Bordeaux glasses (taller, less curved), a couple of champagne flutes, and maybe a few burgundy glasses (more stout and tulip shaped), you're already way ahead of the game. Sneak into your glass collection a smaller version of the Bordeaux glass for white wine and you're officially a cork dork. Honestly, the $3 wineglasses at Ikea are great for the price, versatile, and dishwasher safe.

Useful pro tip: If you think of it, smell the glass before pouring the wine in. If there's any detergent residue or dust you'll pick it up right away, and a quick rinse should clear it up before it meddles with your wine.

wine

Useless pro tip: Make sure the glass is 24 percent full lead crystal. Don't buy into the full lead crystal hype. The level of lead oxide in crystal may increase the clarity and brilliance of the glass, but it also increases the chances that the glass will break if you look at it wrong. A $20 hand-wash-only glass offers little to offset the kick to the gut you'll feel when it breaks (and it will).

Removing the Cork

The correct way to remove a cork is simply the fastest, easiest way possible. The tried-and-true corkscrew is a double-level or hinged Pulltap corkscrew with a Teflon-coated worm (the part that screws into the cork). You will never need another one, and any decent wine shop will have them for sale. The popular rabbit or screwpull-style openers seem easier in theory than in practice, meaning you should actually try one before you buy one (at five to ten times the cost of a Pulltap). That old winged corkscrew we don't remember buying but somehow we all own? Use it for bottle caps and emergencies.

Removing the foil: Of course, before removing the cork we need to remove the foil. You have three options: cutting the foil right above the lip of the bottle, cutting right below the lip, or removing the foil altogether. As long as no part of the foil comes in contact with the wine, it doesn't matter which way you choose, although a cleaner cut is preferred

HOW TO TASTE WINE

to something that looks as if your dog tried to gnaw it off. Plenty of utensils exist to help you through this process, and ideally they should be attached to the corkscrew.

Useful pro tip: If the cork breaks halfway out, carefully go through the process again. Although the cork crumbled in the middle (usually because it dried out), chances are the bottom is still moist and solid because of its contact with the wine. Slowly twist the corkscrew as far as you can into the most intact side of the cork and then slowly begin to extract the last piece of the cork as if it were whole. Pushing the cork into the wine won't ruin the wine, but it might take a bit away from the experience.

The Pour

Right down the middle in an upright glass. Leave the tilted glass for the keg party unless you're pouring champagne, in which case the keg party tilt is appropriate. The pour is when the wine really begins to aerate, so the more aggressive the pour, the better. However, if the wine is older and may have some sediment, you should stand the bottle upright for a few hours before pouring (if no decanter is handy) to let the sediment settle at the bottom, then very slowly pour the wine into the middle of the glass. Sommeliers used to pour wines with the neck of the bottle over candlelight, so they could see when the sediment started to come out. If you're consistently drinking wine with sediment, just invest in a decanter and circumvent all these problems. Pour enough to get one or two good sips and a true example of the color.

Drip collars for wine bottles are one degree removed from sippy cups; don't use them.

Useful pro tip: You may have heard of the half-twist of the wrist at the end of a pour to avoid dripping. Trial and error will dictate how effective you are, but the twist really works once you get the hang of it. Having a napkin handy to wipe the bottle before any drops roll down the outside and soil the label is perfectly fine, as is waiting for the drop to fall in the glass instead of the table. Resting the edge of the bottle on the glass to avoid drips is not.

Check for Cork Taint

Remember when we discussed letting the smells and flavors lead the way rather than your associations? That process doesn't start here. Not yet. Take a quick whiff to see whether you can smell wet, moldy newspaper or paper bags. No need for an in-depth search; you're just looking for a quick yes or no. If it does, the wine might be tainted, or corked, with an undesirable chemical compound (usually the 2,4,6-trichloroanisole [TCA]). The general rule is that 5 to 10 percent of all wine has some form of taint, and if you find your bottle is one of those, feel free to return or refuse it.

HOW TO TASTE WINE

There could be one big problem, however: You have no idea what wet, moldy newspapers smell like.

This is the crux of wine tasting: connecting flavors and smells with associations. But what happens when no association exists? Wine experts love to throw out esoteric correlations that usually alienate rather than illuminate ("subtle hints of gooseberries and stone fruit"). How many people know what gooseberries and stone fruit actually are, let alone smell and taste like?

Unless you've had the misfortune of a flooded basement or a rainy-day visit to the recycling center, you probably can't conjure up the scent of wet newspapers. Fortunately, one man's wet newspapers are another man's wet cardboard, or another man's wet dog. Although the chemical compound may be the same, the association will vary from person to person. Go with whichever association rings most true with you.

Of course, you could grab a bunch of newspapers or paper bags, soak them, and let them get moldy. Or if you're in a restaurant or with a group of friends and someone identifies a wine as corked, ask for a big glass of it and go to town. Stick your nose in there and take some huge whiffs. Go ahead and drink it if you'd like; the wine may taste bad but won't make you sick. Most important, remember it. This association is definitely a good one to have, because you'll use it every time you try wine. Whether it smells of wet cardboard or moldy firewood to you, as long as you can identify cork taint in a wine you'll be in good shape.

wine

Useful pro tip: Make your cork taint decision immediately. Your olfactory senses will immediately adjust to the cork taint chemical compound, and the more you second-guess, the less pronounced the odor becomes. Don't worry; cork taint odor returns with a vengeance once the wine is allowed to breathe. Your goal as a taster is to make sure it never gets the chance.

Useless pro tip: Pouring the wine into a plastic bag or a bowl lined with plastic wrap will pull the cork taint out of the wine. It's a good bar trick and at least chemically viable, but cork taint not only creates an undesirable odor but actually saps the wine of its natural aromas and flavors. Removing the cork taint would just leave you with a flat, tasteless wine. Accept your loss and move on.

Check the Temperature

We're still leading with our associations. Taste the wine solely to see whether the temperature is out of the ordinary. You're looking to see whether the wine is too cold (doesn't taste like much of anything) or too warm (tastes like alcohol). A common misconception is that red wines should be room temperature and whites should be cold. More accurately, red wine should be cool and white wine a bit cooler. Temperature will drastically change the balance of aromas in a wine, so before passing judgment be sure to check the wine and adjust it accordingly.

How to Taste Wine

Useful pro tip: Chill your reds. Throwing your red wines in the refrigerator just before opening them can be a great idea. Remember that the bottle itself will chill before the wine inside does, so always leave it in a bit longer than you think you'll need. If the wine becomes too cold, it will warm back up quickly after you pour it in your glass. It's always easier to warm up a cold wine in your glass than cool down a warm one.

The Swirl

The wine is flawless and at the perfect temperature in your glass. Now you need to wake it up and get it ready for tasting. Aerate the wine by swirling it in your glass as vigorously as you can manage. If you don't know how to swirl, then try the following: Set your wineglass on a table and grab the stem as if it were a pen. Now, with your imaginary pen begin to draw little circles, about the size of a dime, on the table. After a few circles you'll see the wine swirling in your glass. Now gradually grow the circles to the size of a nickel, and then a quarter, but keep the same speed and rhythm. The larger the circles, the faster the wine will swirl around. Eventually you won't need the table anymore.

wine

The Visual
More important in blind tastings, the look of a wine tells a lot, such as its origin, maturity, and alcohol content. Fortunately, most of that information is on the label, so there's no need to play guessing games. Because different wines mature at different paces, checking the color will confirm how far along in its lifespan the wine is. The "legs" or "tears" of a wine have less to do with a wine's quality and more to do with its viscosity, or how much alcohol and sugar it has. The brighter, more vibrant the color the younger the wine, and a duller, brown or orange tinge indicates age.

The Sniff
Finally! Immediately after you get a good swirl going and release all those great aromas into the air, stick your nose into the glass as far as it goes. Inhale and smell. Remember, don't go looking for smells someone told you to find. Actually, don't go looking at all. Go finding! Find as your nose finds a barbecue on a summer day or low tide a mile before you actually see it. You may need to try it a few times before something starts to pop out. Don't be surprised if it reminds you of some off-the-wall things.

HOW TO TASTE WINE

Useful pro tip: Let your body inhale for you. Believe it or not, sometimes people are so distracted by inhaling that they forget to smell altogether. Your body inhales and exhales on its own quite efficiently, so let it do most of the work for you. Rather than suck in air through your nostrils, exhale as much air as you can before smelling your wine. At that last moment when your body reminds you it's out of air, stick your nose in the glass and relax, letting your body naturally inhale through your nose. This way, you can focus less on the breathing and more on the aromas.

Useless pro tip: Exhale through your nose to activate your "retrotaste." Not to be confused with aftertaste, which is both the persistence of taste in the mouth and the introduction of information from taste buds in our soft palate and back of the throat, "retrotaste" is the notion that we continue to smell even after swallowing. Although it's true, there's no need to bend over backward in an attempt to extract more information. The goal is to streamline the process of smell, not encumber it with extra steps. Do what you know and skip this.

wine

The Taste

Interesting enough, the sense of taste in our palate is limited to bitter, salty, sweet, sour, and umami (loosely translated as "savory"). Secondary evaluations such as astringency (dryness) and viscosity (thickness) also happen on the palate and relate directly to wine. But all those flavors pertaining to wine aren't really flavors but the combination of aromas and mouthfeel, or the interplay between our sense of smell and sense of taste. The passion fruit you "tasted" in your Sauvignon Blanc is predominately a smell, not a taste.

It may take a few sips before your palate adjusts to a particular acidic or tannic wine. Likewise, depending on what else you've ingested your palate may be skewed toward an acidic bias or a fatty craving. Simply put, the goal of a wine's mouthfeel is to be balanced across all facets of taste, either independently (a standalone glass of wine) or as part of a greater experience (as in a food and wine pairing). A couple of sips may be necessary to calibrate your palate, but you should be able to determine whether you find the wine too sweet, dry, astringent, or bitter.

How to Taste Wine

Repeat

Practice really does make perfect when it comes to tasting wine. Fortunately, you don't need to identify everything just from one sip. Keep taking more sips until you feel you've found everything the wine has to offer. A great wine will continue to evoke new and interesting flavors with each new sip. Once you learn (relearn?) to let your senses lead the way, accessing your catalog of flavors and associations becomes easier. Soon you'll be able to identify all sorts of different flavors and aromas in different types of wines. Ultimately you'll be able to answer the big wine question: "Why do I really like this?" Knowing why will help you choose, buy, and enjoy wine while still remaining enchanted and smitten every time you pop a cork.

ns gs# buying wine

buying wine

For some reason the act of buying wine, whether in a store or in a restaurant, induces an inordinate level of anxiety for many people. The anxiety boils down to two specific concerns:

- I don't want to be swindled.

- If I buy a bad wine, my knowledge and appreciation will forever be questioned.

Some shoppers refuse the help of sommeliers or store employees for fear that they'll be hustled into a bottle beyond their price range and appreciation. In this chapter we'll discuss the business of wine and how to understand and benefit from it when you purchase wine in restaurants or at retail establishments.

wine

Understanding the Wine Business

Understanding how a bottle of wine finds its way to market can be helpful in understanding how that same bottle ultimately carries a particular price.

Since Prohibition, the liquor business has incorporated a three-tier system intended to protect producers and consumers alike. This system allows tax collection at each level while avoiding any monopolies along the way. The three tiers are as follows:

Tier 1: Producers

This level includes both the wineries and the importers (for foreign wineries) that represent them. Each producer has the expenditures of vineyard management, production, bottling, warehousing, and marketing of the wine. Some producers, such as *négociants* in Burgundy or cooperative wineries, divide these responsibilities and buy already-grown grapes (or even already-made wine) and pick up the process midway from bottling, marketing, and sales. Either way, enough income must be generated to cover all the costs of production with enough profit left over to compensate workers at all stages of production, from the shareholders of a large multinational conglomerate down to the temporary grape pickers brought in at harvest.

Maintaining any winery requires a consistent, reliable income every year. However, consistency is far from the norm in the wine industry. Say a winery in Italy counts on

BUYING WINE

$1 million in sales from the United States every year, but in one year the exchange rate between the euro and the dollar deteriorates to the point that $1 million is worth half the euros it was the year before. Either the winery figures out a way to sell twice as much, or it charges twice as much for the same bottle. Or take a California winery whose business is based on an expensive Cabernet consistently rated at 93 points (more on scores later), only to have an off year when the wine isn't nearly as good and gets a much lower score. Because no one will buy the wine at the price of its predecessors, the winery has to either discount the wine or find some other way to offset the disparity in price and quality. Wineries can't sit on a vintage forever; they need the barrels and space for next year's selections.

Obviously these levels of inconsistency would be too risky for any business, which is why wineries maintain lines of credit with banks, buy monetary futures to hedge their bets against financial downturns, and have varying tiers of wine at different prices, of which, depending on the vintage, they can make more or less. The point is, these instances will ultimately trickle down to the consumer level and affect you and what you pay. Don't worry, you need not scour harvest reports and exchange rates before you look at a wine list, but it may be comforting to know that all these considerations come into play when a wine is priced.

Tier 2: Wholesalers and Distributors

Wholesalers are the reliable middlemen who get the wine from the winery to the store or restaurant and, in turn, get a cut. The competition between distributors ensures the variety and availability of different wines at different prices to the consumer. For a winery looking to sell their wine in a particular region, aligning with a distributor with a preexisting sales force, warehouse, and delivery fleet usually is less expensive than mounting an independent distribution project of their own.

Because distributors usually take the same markups (anywhere from 20 to 30 percent), you may wonder exactly how they affect you, the consumer. Because the distributor's salespeople are the direct connection to retail and wine buyers, wineries do their best to train and incentivize these salespeople to sell their wine. A distributor's salesperson may have hundreds of wineries in his or her portfolio but a finite number of points of sale (stores and restaurants) and a set number of hours in a week to sell to them. Therefore, salespeople choose which wines to sell based on three criteria:

Quotas: When a winery teams up with a distributor, it does so with certain sales expectations. Perhaps the winery is switching to a new distributor, so they have historical sales figures from the previous one. Maybe the distributor, when courting the winery's business, promised a certain number of cases sold. Whatever the agreement, the distributor usually sets quotas for wineries to make sure the sales numbers come in at the end of the year. Bonus money and job security depend on hitting these quotas, so salespeople will hit those quotas, regardless of whether they even like the wine.

Incentives: Many wineries offer sales incentives to salespeople to encourage them to sell their wine. Those incentives could be everything from a monetary bonus per case (say, $10 to $20 extra per case on top of the standard commission) to all-expense-paid trips to visit the winery upon reaching a certain number of cases in a certain time. These incentives are where the real money is for a distributor salesperson, so one can't blame them for trying to hit as many as possible. If a salesperson has to choose between two different Chardonnays to sell and one of them has a $10 per case incentive that covers his child's piano lessons for the month, then the choice is easy. Incentives are a great way for wineries to deplete inventories quickly and control the efforts and mindshare of the distributor's sales force.

Merit: Although quotas and incentives are an unfortunate reality of the wine business, plenty of wines are still sold based on their value and quality alone. Distributors' salespeople are usually well trained and want to take care of their customers as well as possible. The relationship between salesperson and buyer is the most important part of the wine business, and the more honest and sincere the transactions, the closer the relationship is likely to be. Not every wine salesperson is a mercenary.

Tier 3: Retailers and Restaurants

Finally, the wine has reached the place where you and I can go and buy it. Depending on their clientele, the store or restaurant will buy accordingly. A tiny bodega catering to a low-income customer may not have any wine over $10 in their store, whereas a fine wine shop in a posh suburb may not carry anything below $10. Almost all wines have a discount depending on the quantity purchased, so that little bodega may devote its whole budget to buying ten cases of a lower-end wine to get the best price available. The fine wine shop will spread that budget around and buy one case each of ten different wines to provide the quality and selection their customers desire.

As far as markups go, usually a retailer will mark up wines 50 percent and a restaurant 200 percent, so a bottle of wine wholesaling for $20 will sell in a store for $30 and on a restaurant's wine list for $60. Also, restaurants usually pour wines by the glass for the price they pay for the bottle, so a $10 glass of Pinot Noir probably costs the restaurant $10 a bottle. At five glasses of wine per bottle, that Pinot Noir brings in a profit of $40 per bottle, or $480 per case. All that profit balances out the other costs that eat away at restaurant profits, such as daily non-kitchen expenses.

BUYING WINE

Buying Wine in a Store
Now that you know a bit about the business of wine, it's time to figure out how to use that information when buying wine. Before that happens, you need to figure out what kind of wine shopper you are. Most people fall into three loyalty categories: labels, recommendations, and deals. Knowing which one you're in will help you get the best wine for the best price.

Label Loyal
Wine drinkers who are label loyal usually make a beeline to the same wine every time. It's like buying deodorant: No matter what store you're in, you head to the section and scan all the choices until you find the exact one you've been using. In fact, all the other choices just get in the way, don't they?

Buying tips:

- **Don't ever be embarrassed.** If you go somewhere that scoffs when you ask for your favorite wine or tries to convince you how bad your taste is, turn around and walk out. That type of negativity gives wine a bad name, and plenty of other places will happily take your business.

wine

- **Buy at the big stores.** The bigger chains such as Walmart, Costco, and regional supermarkets offer such a large chunk of business that producers, importers, and distributors all work at a smaller profit just to guarantee their spot. The buying power of those chains (including state-run liquor outlets such as those in New Hampshire and Pennsylvania) almost guarantees the best price and availability, so if you're fortunate enough to drink a wine available at one of these places, take full advantage. The cozy, well-decorated, and knowledgeable fine wine store may make you feel special, but they probably can't compete on price.

- **Buy by the case.** Sure, it may seem like a big chunk of change at the time, but some stores offer discounts of 10 to 20 percent if you buy a full case of wine. Not only do you save money, you save time spent going to the wine store. Invited to a last-minute dinner party? You already have something to bring. Hosting a last-minute dinner party? You already have something to serve. Over the course of a healthy wine-drinking lifetime those savings add up, and (usually) the wine will keep for as long as you need it to.

BUYING WINE

Recommendation Loyal

These wine buyers rely on the suggestions of both advertisements and employees. Companies spend millions of dollars to produce shelf-talkers (those little paper ads right next to the bottle on the shelf) proclaiming the latest 90-point score or press accolade. Whether from the "authorities" such as Robert Parker or *Wine Spectator* or just the owner of the shop, you've decided to let the experts choose for you.

Buying tips:

- **Look for coordinated displays and deals.** If a wine has recently scored well in a publication, importers and distributors will splash out the cash to make sure they turn that good press into sales. Usually that cash means better pricing all the way down the line, ending up in your pocket. However, make sure they don't bait you with a good score only to switch you to a wine from a different vintage.

- **Just because a wine doesn't have a score doesn't mean it's bad.** More wines exist than wine critics can review. Just because Wine A got reviewed and Wine B didn't doesn't mean Wine A is better; it's just more fortunate (and perhaps better connected). By purchasing only wines with reviews from major publications, you limit yourself to a small selection of wines. Feel free to ask the wine buyers

wine

in the store why they bought a particular wine for the store. Their response (or review, if you will) may be just as valuable as any numerical score.

- **Old news is not good news.** Let's say a Sauvignon Blanc receives a Best Buy rating from a magazine upon the wine's release. Three years later, you see the same wine, with the same score, for a great price. However, that Sauvignon Blanc is nowhere near the same as when it was first scored. Higher-quality wines will have staying power (and even get better with age), but be wary of the "value picks." Many of these "best wines under $10" and the like are scored with the caveat that they be consumed soon, and in this instance companies and retailers are banking on their recommendation-loyal customers to help clean up this inventory for them.

- **Scores and reviews should add value to the wine, not cost.** Be careful of stores that raise the price on wines receiving great scores. Granted, perhaps the importer or distributor raised the price and the store had no option but to comply. To many people in the wine business, each great score or review comes with a "cha-ching!" If you see a hastily scribbled price increase accompanying a good score, beware.

BUYING WINE

- **Buy by the case to take advantage of full-case discounts.** Some stores will give you a discount for mixing and matching twelve bottles together if you can't afford twelve of the same bottle. If you see a wine with a great score at a great price, there's a chance it will sell out. Buy a bunch; you won't regret it.

Deal Loyal

We've discussed some deals and their reasons already, but the true bargain seeker must be ready to ask a lot of questions. Remember, rarely will the retailer not make his or her 50 percent markup, so wineries, importers, and distributors wholly support almost all these sales:

Good deals: The following are good reasons a wine might be on sale:

- Introduction to the region or market: Brand-new wines will offer great pricing to get in the stores.

- Marketing push: Dollars spent to capitalize on a good score, advertising, or other marketing plan (e.g., rebates, coupons) will lower the price of a wine.

- Quotas: Importers and distributors will do what it takes to hit their sales numbers.

wine

- Incentives: Someone, somewhere is getting something nice in exchange for all these cases at this great price.

- Overstock: Too much wine and too little demand means a big cut in price to free up barrels or warehouse space for the next vintage.

- Discontinued: When a winery or importer stops doing business with a distributor, usually the distributor will discount a wine (sometimes selling at cost) just to get it out of the building.

Bad deals: Stay away from these tempting but deceptive discounts:

- Last legs: Selling out a wine before it goes bad happens more than you think. The lower the price + the older the wine = the greater the risk.

- Line extensions: Taking in all the wines from a winery just to get the better price on the one or two wines that are actually good also happens more than you think. If you see a wine being treated like the redheaded stepchild to its brethren in a display, it's because it actually is. Stay away.

- Half-off: There are plenty of inflated prices out there. Look at what the price is rather than what it was.

- Bins: Bin wines are advertised as great values, but stores usually make *more* money on them than other wines in the store. That means you're paying more than you should.

A quick word about independently owned fine wine shops: Almost everyone who goes through the trouble of opening and maintaining a fine wine shop absolutely loves wine and everything about it. They pride themselves on selecting the best wines for the best price and do the best they can to compete with the big boys. If possible, try to support these shops, as the care and attention given to the selection will usually be given to you as well. These shops are great environments to ask questions, try new wines, and build a rapport with people willing to share their passion. Isn't that worth a few bucks more here and there?

wine

Buying Wine in a Restaurant

More than ever before, people are drinking wine in restaurants. Wine bars are popping up everywhere, and what used to be an afterthought (the wine list) is now prominently featured. Keeping in mind the restaurant markups (charging three times the cost by the bottle and charging the bottle cost for each glass), here are some tips to consider when ordering:

- Buy by the bottle if you can. Increasingly, restaurants are milking the profits from their by-the-glass program. That means bringing in less expensive wine and charging more for it. Plenty of restaurants actually charge more per glass than what they pay per bottle. If you're with a friend, can agree on a bottle, and expect to drink at least two glasses each, then ordering by the bottle will save you money. As a rule, the fifth glass in each bottle works out to be free. If you can buy a wine by the bottle that's also offered by the glass, consider it, because the restaurant probably buys that wine in multiple cases and gets a discount. If you're lucky, they've incorporated that discounted price and passed along the savings to you. Also, more and more restaurants now have rules allowing you to take the remainder of a bottle home with you. Be sure to ask a server or sommelier about this, and take advantage if possible.

- The sweet spot for bottles on a wine list begins around $40. Remember, that $40 bottle sells in a store for about $20, and there are plenty of great bottles at that price.

BUYING WINE

- Use the sommelier and forgo the server. In this day of cutting costs, the sommelier position has become endangered. However, if you are in a restaurant with a sommelier or wine steward working the floor, be sure to pick his or her brain. There's no need to impress either; the clearer you are with your questions (including budget), the more they can help you choose and appreciate a wine. The servers have only short-term knowledge about the wine list, because they learn about three to five wines a week if they're lucky. Considering the high turnover of servers in most restaurants, that's usually a small percentage of the wine list. Servers will recommend what they know, and usually they don't know enough (no offense to servers out there). However, you must tip your server on any wine you order.

- Consider paying corkage and bring your own. You probably never have done it, and often it's not mentioned on the list, but if you call ahead and ask whether the restaurant allows you to bring in your own wine and how much the corkage fee is, you'll be pleasantly surprised. Most places without a liquor license will let you bring in wines for free, and other places with a license and a wine list will generally charge around $20. Assuming the restaurant would charge twice what you paid in the store, it's worth it to buy a $30 bottle in a store and bring it with you.

wine

- Wine flights are a great way to try different wines, but don't make an evening of them. Many people think flights of wine are like tapas: small portions of different flavors that, after a bunch of them, leave you satisfied. However, wine flights are expensive on a cost-per-ounce basis, and unless you're really paying attention and actively tasting them, they're not worth the cost.

- Stay away from house wines: These wines are like well liquors in a bar. Ask a bartender for a vodka tonic, and unless you specifically mention a top-shelf vodka, you'll usually get the cheap stuff in the plastic bottle. Same with wine in some places. If you're just having a glass, take a quick look at the list and order something by name. Otherwise, there's no telling what you're getting.

- If you like to order sangria, then you're paying for the biggest con at the bar. Would you pay $10 a glass for Two-Buck Chuck with cheap brandy, sugar, and a few orange slices? That's exactly what it is. If you're lucky, the wine in the sangria is from all the bottles that have been opened too long and can't be served by the glass anymore. More often than not, it's box or jug wine.

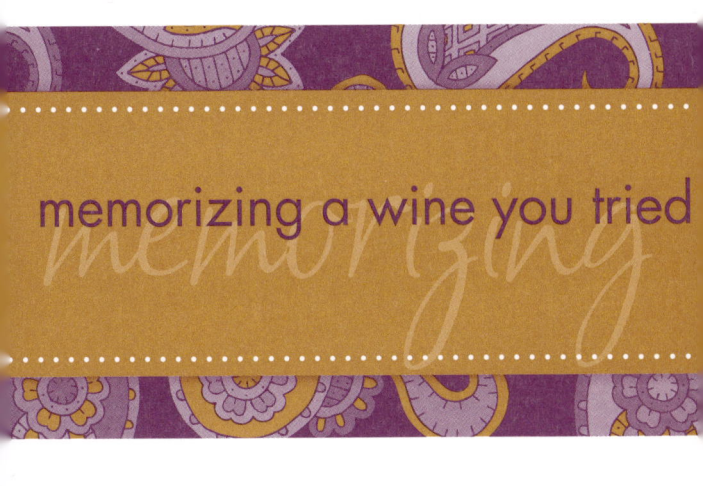

memorizing a wine you tried

memorizing a wine you tried

Remember, your loyalties are to what you like to drink rather than who made it. There are three things you should try to commit to memory when you try a wine you'd like to remember. Look for them in this particular order:

- **Grape:** First and foremost, be sure to find out what grape it is. Sure, it sounds like common sense, but in the heat of the moment most people will scan a wine label like they do a page in a book; top to bottom, left to right. Ignore everything else and go straight for the grape. Odds are you liked that particular wine because of the grape and much less the winemaker or region. It's like ordering your favorite Chinese dish: You know you love the General Tso's from your local joint, but you find yourself at a Chinese restaurant on the other side of town. What are you ordering? The General Tso's. It may be a little better or a little worse, but it's close enough to still reliably enjoy. Same thing with wine: Knowing what grape you like sets up a safe zone for the next time you need to buy.

wine

- **Region:** Sometimes those labels are pretty confusing, and instead of a grape you just see a region such as Barolo or Pommard. That's actually all the info you'll need, because those regions produce wines made of Nebbiolo and Pinot Noir grapes, respectively. Walking into a wine shop and asking for these regions will get you a wine with very similar characteristics. If the store doesn't have Barolo (which is rare), they could offer another Nebbiolo-based wine (such as Barbaresco) or a similar wine from Piedmont but a different grape (such as Barbera). If the store doesn't carry a Pommard, at least they know you're looking for a Pinot Noir from Burgundy and can suggest another village wine from the Côte de Beaune and at worst another Pinot Noir. Tell a store you had a great red from Bordeaux and they immediately know it was probably a blend of Cabernet Sauvignon and Merlot. Ideally, remember the region by country, then subregion, then anything else you can remember (e.g., United States, Napa Valley, Oakville, or Italy, Tuscany, Montalcino).

- **Price:** It may sound cheap, but knowing the value of what you drank may determine what you buy more than anything. If you were fortunate enough to drink a $100 bottle of red Bordeaux but want to spend only $20 a bottle on something similar, you may enjoy a $20 Old World–style Bordeaux blend from Chile much more than an actual $20 Bordeaux. A wine's quality can be just as satisfying as

memorizing a wine you tried

any flavor or feature. If quality drives your palate, be sure to keep that in mind when buying because the quality-to-price ratio can differ wildly from one bottle to another.

Only after memorizing those three things should you look to memorize the winery. A funny story about memorizing wineries first: I struck up a wine conversation with a woman at a party, who proceeded to tell me all about her favorite Italian wine producer (whose name she couldn't quite recall) and how she and her husband were currently drinking this winery's Zinfandel. Considering that most Italian wineries don't make Zinfandel (the closest would be Primitivo in the southeastern part of the country), I was quite curious. She assured me it was quite rare indeed, as she often went looking for it in the Italian sections of wine shops and never saw it either. With my interest piqued and no progress in figuring out this mystery winery, she offered to call her husband to find out. Thirty minutes later, she found me again and exclaimed, "Coppola winery! It's Francis Coppola winery." Francis Ford Coppola is a fairly large and well-known winery in California (not to mention a renowned film director), but she and her husband just looked at the label, saw the name *Coppola*, and assumed the wine was Italian. An easy mistake to make, a lesson learned, and a good laugh to boot.

Just as the grape, region, and price will help you remember the wine you liked, a few other things will actually lead you astray. The following things are not criteria to remember:

wine

- **Vintage:** Unless you're a bona-fide collector, vintages have the least to do with why you like the wine. Too many people put too much stock into the vintage of the wine they like. For the majority of New World (non-European) wines, variation from year to year is negligible, and modern winemaking practices and market supply and demand keep Old World wine production more consistent than ever. For example, the much-heralded 2007 vintage in the Rhône Valley in France created such a demand that many dismissed the 2006 vintage altogether, forgoing some fantastic wines and prices in the process. Think of a great vintage as an added bonus, not a determining factor.

- **Label:** "I had this great bottle last night. The label was blue, with some stars and this yellow writing on the side." No. Please don't.

storing wine

storing wine

Many casual wine drinkers are convinced that older is necessarily better. But you need to define the term better for yourself. Two things happen as a wine ages:

- **A wine's aromas change.** As mentioned earlier, a wine has three classified aromas: primary, secondary, and tertiary. When a wine is young, the primary aromas dominate, with a fruity and vibrant exuberance. The secondary aromas are there but masked and overwhelmed. As the primary aromas fade with time, the secondary aromas become more evident, and its tertiary aromas (derived from age) increase as well. In a perfect world, a wine reaches a moment where its primary, secondary, and tertiary aromas are all present, balanced, and together create a unique and complex bouquet.

- **A wine's tannins and acidity diminish.** Tannins and acidity give wine its life, so the older a wine, the lower levels of acidity and tannins you will find. For big red wines such as Cabernet Sauvignon, for example, the tannin level may be so high when young that the wine will be undrinkable. Letting a wine age allows those tannins to relax and soften, making the wine much more approachable. Also, just like aromas, the grape tannins (usually the strongest and most aggressive) fade first, allowing the softer tannins (from barrel aging, for example) to remain.

So why wouldn't you try to hold on to every wine until it reaches the perfect peak moment? Because almost all wineries release their wines when they believe they can be enjoyed immediately, meaning that they do a lot of this work for you already. The majority of wine is ready to drink as soon as it hits the shelves, so keep that in mind.

The best way to circumvent the whole question of aging wine is to purchase multiple bottles of the same wine. Because we already discussed buying wine by the case, you should have multiples of the same wine with which to experiment. Drink one right away to taste it (and satisfy your curiosity at the same time). A Beaujolais Nouveau will taste

storing wine

completely different after a few months, but a great Bordeaux may actually taste worst after a year (some of the best wines go through a hibernation phase as they gear up for a long life). Some wines, such as inexpensive Sauvignon Blancs, may lose their acidity before the secondary aromas even appear, in which case the younger the wine the better. If you know you like fruity wines, keep in mind that the fruit will be the first thing to go.

Many casual wine drinkers own some sort of wine refrigerator, which works great but isn't really necessary. Some things to avoid:

- Huge temperature swings. If you keep wine in a garage that's 40 degrees in the winter and 80 in the summer, find somewhere else.

- Consistent temperature but too cold (below 45 degrees) or too hot (above 75).

- Direct sunlight or fluorescent light.

- Storing real cork–enclosed bottles upright for long periods of time (the cork will dry out).

wine

The guidelines hold true for all wines, but in practice they depend on the wine itself. Are you storing a $200 case of wine for a month or a $2,000 case of wine for a decade? If the storing and laying down of a wine plays a big role in the "business plan" of the purchase, then the guidelines quickly become rules not to be broken. Proper storage, or lack thereof, determines a huge part of a collectible wine's value when it comes time to auction it off.

Unfortunately, the best lesson about aging wine happens when you've held onto a bottle for a bit too long. Maybe you forgot all about it, or maybe you saved it for a special occasion that never happened. Whatever the case, the wine has lost its color, fruit, and acidity; simply put, it's too old and tired. If you think it might be time to open a special wine before it's too late but no special occasion is around the corner, make opening that wine its own special occasion. Invite over a few friends who appreciate it to share in your experience (and in turn be invited to their places when they do likewise), set out a simple spread of food (nothing that'll compete with the wine for attention), and enjoy! Remember, a wine in the glass is worth two in the rack.

food and wine pairings

food and wine pairings

In this day of smartphones and laptops, many people want quicker answers to fewer questions. Hundreds of food and wine pairing applications are now a few clicks away. To many, a perfect food and wine pairing guide will churn out a formulaic response ("If eating x, then drink y or z"), sufficiently answering questions and shedding accountability at the same time. For something as subjective and personal as wine, food and wine pairings have become shockingly black and white, right and wrong. Let's take a step back and look at some of the fundamentals seemingly lost in the shuffle.

Complementary Versus Supplementary

Keeping in mind that our perception of a taste combines aromas with mouthfeel, food and wine pairings can be complementary, in which the food and wine offer similar features, or supplementary, in which the food and wine offer completely different features lacking in the other. Many times the best pairing occurs when one identifies which of these should take precedence, but knowing which one takes a bit of science.

wine

Remember the five things your tongue can actually pick up: bitter, salty, sweet, sour, and umami (savory). Wine covers three of those: bitter (tannins), sweet (residual sugar), and sour (acidity). That leaves our tongues looking for salty, savory things to complete the experience. The primary exchange occurs between the sugar from the wine and the salt from the meal supplement, creating a much more interesting and multifaceted experience on the palate.

With the sugars and salts dancing around each other, the tannins and acidity are searching for their pairings. The tannins are pretty straightforward: They'll attach to proteins and fats, if available, or to your tongue if nothing else is around. Without wine, fats and proteins envelop your palate and coat it, dulling your sense of taste. Without fats or proteins, the tannins bind to proteins in your saliva and envelop your palate and coat it, giving you a dry mouth and bitter taste. The symbiotic, supplementary relationship between tannins, fats, and proteins keeps your palate clean and exposes it to more sense receptors, and once proteins are broken down into amino acids, the savory sensors are triggered.

When in wine alone, acidity supplements the sugar in wine and balances it out. However, wine acidity has a *complementary* relationship with acidity in food, meaning you want to *match* acidity rather than counteract it. So a high-acid meal such as salad with dressing or tomato sauce requires an equally high-acid wine. If you pair a low-acid wine with a high-acid meal, your wine will barely register on the palate

FOOD AND WINE PAIRINGS

and taste more like water than anything else. Pair a high-acid wine with a low-acid meal and you'll want to add more acid to the meal (e.g., squeezing a lemon over it) or neutralize some of that acidity with more salt.

Lastly, the alcohol in wine determines a wine's viscosity, or body. Match a wine's body with the weight of the dish. Keep in mind that alcohol accentuates the effects of spices, including salt.

Because a discussion about food and wine pairings wouldn't be complete without charts, here is a helpful chart summarizing the relationships (either directly related, as in high acidity + high acidity, or indirectly related, as in high sugar + low tannins):

	Food				
Wine	**Proteins and Fats**	**Acidity**	**Sugar**	**Salt**	**Weight**
Tannins	Directly	Neutral	Indirectly	Directly	Directly
Acidity	Directly	Directly	Indirectly	Directly	Directly
Sugar	Neutral	Indirectly	Directly	Directly	Neutral
Alcohol	Directly	Indirectly	Directly	Indirectly	Directly

And, finally, a list of wine varietals and their standard characteristics:

White Wine	Tannins	Acidity	Sugar	Alcohol
Albariño	Low	High	Medium	Low
Chardonnay	Medium	Medium	Medium	High
Chenin Blanc	Low	High	High	Medium
Garganega	Low	Medium	Medium	Medium
Gewürztraminer	Low	Medium	Medium	Medium
Grüner Veltliner	Low	High	Low	Medium
Muscadet	Low	High	High	Low
Muscat	Low	High	High	Low
Pinot Blanc	Low	Low	Low	High
Pinot Grigio (Pinot Gris)	Low	Low	Medium	Medium
Riesling	Low	High	High	Low
Sauvignon Blanc	Low	High	Medium	Medium
Trebbiano	Low	High	Low	Low
Viognier	Low	Low	Low	High

Food and Wine Pairings

Red Wine	Tannins	Acidity	Sugar	Alcohol
Barbera	Low	High	Medium	Medium
Cabernet Franc	Medium	Medium	Medium	Medium
Cabernet Sauvignon	High	Medium	Medium	High
Carmenere	Medium	Medium	High	Medium
Dolcetto	Low	Low	Low	Low
Gamay	Low	High	High	Low
Grenache	Medium	High	High	Medium
Malbec	Medium	Low	High	High
Merlot	Medium	Medium	Medium	Medium
Mourvèdre	High	High	Medium	High
Nebbiolo	High	High	Low	High
Pinotage	Medium	High	High	Low
Pinot Noir	Low	Medium	Medium	Low
Sangiovese	High	High	Low	Low
Shiraz or Syrah	High	High	High	High
Tempranillo	Medium	Medium	Low	Medium
Touriga Nacional	High	Medium	High	High
Zinfandel	Medium	High	High	High

wine

Of course, all these generalizations have their exceptions. For example, the difference between a supple, austere Argentinean Malbec and racy, bright one from Cahors is striking. A clean, un-oaked French Chablis, which is 100 percent Chardonnay, barely resembles its buttery, oaky California counterparts. A grape grown in a cooler climate will usually have more acidity and less sugar than the same grape grown in a warmer climate.

Back to the Basics
All the wine pairing rules you learned in Wine 101 still hold true for the most part: white with fish, red with red meat, match the color of the wine to the color of the food, and so on. The tannins in red wine still taste awful when mixed with fish oils in your mouth. Italian wine still goes best with Italian food, dessert wine with desserts, and a big red wine with a juicy steak. Now you know *why* certain pairings work and others don't. Putting together a wine pairing based on the qualities of each item and not some phone application will make you appreciate it that much more. You'll never look at food and wine the same way again.

organic, biodynamic, and sulfite-free crazes

organic, biodynamic, and sulfite-free crazes

We've all heard it before: Someone refuses a glass of red wine because "The sulfites give me a headache" or "I'm allergic, so I only drink sulfite-free wine." Coincidentally, the organic food boom hit the wine trade at the same time as these allergies (where were all these sulfite allergies fifty years ago?), promising lower sulfites, better growing practices, and better overall wine. But is it really worth it?

Sulfites

Sulfur occurs in nature and has been used for thousands of years. Egyptians and Romans used sulfur to clean and sterilize, a practice some wineries still use today (would you rather they use bleach?). About three hundred years ago the use of sulfur as a preservative in food began, and it expanded during the war years of the early twentieth century as armies tried to figure out the best way to send food to the front lines without spoilage. This practice peaked in the 1960s and 1970s, as families welcomed TV dinners and salad bars became a popular staple of cafeterias and restaurants. Sulfur dioxide inhibits the browning of produce (such as lettuce) and therefore gives that produce a longer life on the salad bar.

The abuse of sulfur as a preservative led to the first wave of sulfur-related allergic reactions, causing the FDA to regulate the use of sulfur in the mid-1980s and mandating the now-common "Contains Sulfites" disclaimer on anything above a certain level.

Aside from sterilization, wineries used sulfur (in the form of copper sulfate) as a cure-all for fungi and other diseases in the vineyard. These days the need for pesticides in the vineyard has decreased as science and technology (not to mention trial and error) have helped vineyard managers keep their vines and grapes disease free. Whereas vineyard workers used to spray sulfur on recently picked grapes to prevent spoilage on the trip to the winery, more and more now spray carbon dioxide (much like the wine-preserving spray cans you can buy to spray into an open bottle, creating a blanket of carbon dioxide covering the wine that prevents oxygen from coming into contact with it). However, the use of sulfur dioxide in the winemaking process, in many ways, continues to be as important as ever. Sulfur dioxide functions in two crucial ways:

- **Antimicrobial:** Given the nature of microbes and bacteria, they're certain to find their way into wine either intentionally (as used in malolactic fermentation) or unintentionally (such as *Brettanomyces* and other wine-destroying bacteria). In turn, winemakers will

Organic, Biodynamic, and Sulfite-Free Crazes

use sulfur dioxide both actively (to stop the process of malolactic fermentation exactly when they get the desired level) and preventively (to kill any bacteria that have infiltrated the wine).

- **Antioxidative:** Oxygen will break down (and "brown") a wine just as it browns lettuce. Exposed to oxygen, wine will oxidate and turn to vinegar within months. Sulfur dioxide binds to any free-floating oxygen molecules and prevents those molecules from binding with and breaking apart the wine.

In short, many winemakers use sulfur dioxide for the same reason sidewalk artists spray hairspray on their charcoal drawings: to preserve the quality without altering it.

So how much sulfur dioxide is necessary? The government measures sulfur dioxide in parts per million as a gas, although it's easier to imagine in its liquid conversion of milligrams per liter. One milligram per liter equates to about 4.5 drops of liquid in a standard 225-liter barrel of wine. Fermentation generates a small amount of sulfur dioxide (roughly 10 to 20 milligrams per liter) as a byproduct, and the U.S. legal limit is 350 milligrams per liter (let's hope you never try a wine with that much). The majority of wines end up with about 80 to 120 milligrams per liter of sulfur dioxide, but it all depends on type and quality of wine. Let's look at some simple examples.

wine

Winemaker A is making a high-quality Cabernet Sauvignon. Her grapes are excellent, with robust tannins and a great acidity. Because tannins, acidity, and alcohol all play a major role in the longevity and natural preservation of the wine, she needs only to stop the malolactic fermentation and add some preventive sulfur dioxide just in case. The result is about 50 milligrams per liter of sulfites.

Winemaker B is making a good-quality Chardonnay. Because it's a Chardonnay, the grape skins won't come in contact with the juice (so the juice stays without color). The wine undergoes plenty of malolactic fermentation to get its buttery mouthfeel, losing some sharp acidity in the process. Aside from the preventive sulfur dioxide, she needs to add more to keep the wine from oxidizing, as the lack of big tannins (from the lack of grape skin contact) and acidity means the wine's natural life span is shorter. The result is about 120 milligram per liter of sulfites.

Winemaker C is making a cheap white wine. The grapes are poor quality, with little acidity and low sugar levels. The mass production of the wine means the conditions are rife with external bacteria. She needs to kill all the bacteria, including any that could accidentally start a malolactic fermentation, because she needs all the acidity she can get. The lack of tannins and acidity means the wine has little natural life span, so she needs the sulfur dioxide to provide it all. The result is about 250 milligrams per liter of sulfites.

Organic, Biodynamic, and Sulfite-Free Crazes

What do these examples mean to you, the wine drinker? Only about 1 percent of the population actually lacks the enzyme that processes sulfites (in other words, is allergic), and those with asthma or aspirin allergies stand the biggest risk of a severe reaction. If you've ever eaten dried fruit (such as dried apricots, which top the sulfite scales at up to ten times the amount in wine) and not had a serious reaction, then you're not one of the unlucky 1 percent. However, by understanding how wineries use sulfur dioxide, you now know the basic rules:

- The better the grapes (with tannins, high acidity, and high sugar levels), the longer the natural life span of the wine and therefore the less sulfur dioxide needed as a preservative.

- White wines usually have more preservative sulfites than reds because reds extract tannins from the grape skins, giving them a longer life span.

- Inoculating a wine with bacteria to undergo malolactic fermentation means you then need to kill the bacteria with sulfur dioxide. Crisp, clean wines meant to be consumed young usually have the least amount of sulfites.

wine

- Sweeter wines have lower acidity and higher sugar levels, making them conducive to bacteria. Winemakers must boost the sulfite level in most sweet wines to prevent infiltration.

Given that sulfites aren't as bad as they're made out to be, you might wonder what the benefit is of drinking a no-sulfite-added wine. Although fragile and short-lived, a wine without added sulfur dioxide can be beautifully expressive and alive if consumed very young. Sulfites sap wine of some of its nuance, which is not a problem if the wine had no nuance to begin with but is definitely a concern for collectible wines. At least now, if you buy a no-sulfite-added wine, you're doing so for the right reasons.

So if you're not allergic to sulfites after all but still get headaches when you drink red wine, what gives? Two things red wines do have more of than white wines are tannins and histamines. After sulfites, tannins are the next popular culprit to blame. If you enjoy tea and coffee, however, tannins aren't the problem, since they're just as common in coffee and tea as they are in wine. That leaves histamines, which affect most people. Although the link has not been directly proven, many consider histamines the most probable cause.

Organic, Biodynamic, and Sulfite-Free Crazes

Histamines can cause a reaction in a variety of ways:

- The alcohol in wine can cause your body to release its own histamines as a defense and bring about the typical allergic reactions of a runny nose, watery eyes, and, in some cases, headaches. If the introduction of histamines overcomes the body's ability to metabolize them (using the enzyme diamine oxidase [DAO]), then an over-the-counter antihistamine can be used to alleviate the symptoms (but not to actually remove the histamines from your system).

- Red wines, along with other foods such as strawberries and fermented foods, have histamines as well. If you can eat high-histamine foods without any reaction but not wine, then the alcohol in wine may be inhibiting the effectiveness of the body's DAO in processing the histamines.

- Wine, processed meats, and other fermented foods (such as cheese) also have tyramines, a kissing cousin to histamines. Likewise, the body has its own kissing cousin to DAO, an enzyme known as monoamine oxidase [MAO], to metabolize tyramines. Unfortunately, many people take MAO inhibitors, otherwise known as antidepressants, leaving the body unable to process tyramine. The resulting buildup of tyramine often results in a headache.

Any of these possibilities could explain why some people have bad reactions to red wine. One person's perfect evening of a charcuterie plate, consisting of cured meats and cheeses, and a glass of red wine could be another person's migraine on a silver platter. Interestingly enough, the body counteracts an overload of histamines by producing adrenaline (just as epinephrine counteracts anaphylactic shock brought on by an allergic reaction). That fluttering heart of yours may have more to do with adrenaline counteracting histamines than the dreamy looks from your date across the table.

Organic and Biodynamic Wines
Seems like most supermarkets now have an organic option for just about everything, with a markup to boot. In some cases, the organic version looks and tastes much better than its conventional counterpart. In other cases, certified organic guarantees a socially responsible production in which all parties, including the environment, are treated fairly and respectfully, without exploitation. Yet other organic items seem exactly the same and perhaps even worse than conventionally produced equivalents. So where does wine fit in?

For many consumers, anything certified organic means it was held to a higher standard and therefore must be better. However, one country's certification may pale in comparison to another. No international certification entity or process

Organic, Biodynamic, and Sulfite-Free Crazes

exists for wine, so a certified organic wine from one country could be more or less organic than an organic wine from somewhere else.

Many organic wineries forgo the certification process because of its long, expensive, and invasive nature. Thousands of dollars and many years are necessary to earn the "Certified Organic" stamp on a label, and no rule exists that if you operate organically you must in turn become certified. In some countries such as France, an inspector could stop by anytime to grab a soil sample and check out the books to see whether anything improper was purchased. If winery owners don't think it's worth the cost and hassle, they won't bother. That means plenty of wineries that could be certified organic actually aren't, and depending on the country, some wineries that aren't certified organic may actually be more organic than other wineries that are.

The quintessential organic wine production involves cultivating grapes without chemical-based pesticides, fungicides, herbicides, and fertilizers. However, many winemakers will tell you that if any of those are necessary to begin with, then you're growing the wrong grapes in the wrong place. From Romans to monks to conquistadors and immigrants, people have continually searched for the best place to plant grape vines with the least amount of problems. Trial and error have determined some of the best grape and location pairings throughout history, pairings that to this day continue to produce excellent grapes without the added use of chemicals. So sacred is this maintenance of grapes and locations that some controlling bodies wouldn't even allow extra water that didn't occur naturally during the season, let alone chemicals. Many winemakers in France and Italy think a more useful approach would be to identify wineries that *aren't* operating organically.

With that in mind, you might assume that most wineries are essentially organic. However, the increase in demand for wine requires an increase in grapes, and with most of the best grape-growing locations already occupied, the ever-expanding vineyards need to go somewhere. It's fairly safe to say that the older vineyard locations produce the most natural (i.e., organic) fruit, and the newer locations may have to chemically compensate for their lack of prime real estate.

A stumbling block on the way to full organic status is the amount of sulfites allowed. As discussed, many winemakers view the addition of sulfur dioxide as a necessity (and some might say a godsend), and too little sulfur dioxide can harm a wine more than too much. Given that the same governing bodies dictating the organic thresholds in wine also oversee produce and other perishables, the sulfur levels determined for organic wines run *very* low (20 parts per million for organic wines in the United States). The stigma of sulfite abuse in the past and the unfair association with other preservatives such as nitrates set the bar too low for most winemakers. Considering that at least half of the 20 parts per million occurs naturally during fermentation, the remainder simply

Organic, Biodynamic, and Sulfite-Free Crazes

isn't enough to produce satisfactory wine. To circumvent the sulfur limit, many wineries opt for the "made with organically grown grapes" distinction, a distinction many wineries in Europe scoff at because they've been growing organic grapes for years.

So maybe certified organic wine isn't all it's meant to be, but it certainly can't be worse, right? Unfortunately, it can. Sometimes, heeding all the strict guidelines for organic certification results in a subpar wine. A winery may decide the marketing gains from organic certification outweigh the noticeable lack of quality; therein lies the concern when buying organic. Be wary of inexpensive, and especially older, organic wines. On the other hand, if the quality of fruit is stellar (as it can be with more upscale organic wineries), then don't hesitate to give it a try.

Some people buy organic when they actually are more concerned with buying sustainably farmed wine. The term *biodynamic* gets thrown around a lot, used interchangeably with *organic* and *sustainable agriculture*. Biodynamic principles trace back to the 1920s and Rudolf Steiner, who supported the notion of a self-contained and sufficient farm as its own organism. Add to that some astrology and a holistic spin, and what was for many years just farming common sense became a full-blown phenomenon. Whether the results of biodynamic farming are better has yet to be proven, but no chemicals of any kind are allowed, and many wineries now certified organic got their starts by following Steiner's biodynamic lead.

Sustainable agriculture, on the other hand, not only includes biodynamic notions of natural intentions and solutions but also requires a socioeconomic and ecological responsibility. Sustainable farms must produce natural products devoid of chemicals while also maintaining the purity of a farm's ecosystem and inhabitants. Recycling, offsetting carbon footprints, and encouraging a return of naturally occurring flora and fauna play a large part in sustainable farms.

So what are your reasons for buying organic, biodynamic, or sustainably farmed wines? Do you specifically want to support wineries that demonstrate a dedication to the environment? Or are you looking for the best possible quality of grape? Maybe you like knowing the wine came from a balanced, peaceful, and natural setting or merely that the wine isn't chock-full of chemicals. Whatever the reason, be sure to remember the differences (and not to assume that nonorganic wines are worse).

so you want to throw a wine party

so you want to throw a wine party

Some might say that wine itself is a party in a bottle, but the more people around to enjoy it, the better. Here are some ideas for throwing a wine party.

Tasting Group

This is by far the most serious of wine parties. Just like a book club, where everyone goes home, reads a book, then meets up to discuss it, here you and your friends do the same. Everyone decides on a wine grape, goes home and studies, then meets up to talk about the grape and try a few examples. You'll need the following:

- Reference materials to read and learn about each grape (the Internet will do fine).

- Wineglasses (multiples per person if possible).

- Wine. Everyone brings one bottle of the same grape. Try to get as many different regions and prices possible. For example, a tasting group of five people studying Sauvignon Blanc could bring a Sauvignon Blanc from the Loire Valley, Bordeaux, California, Chile, and New Zealand.

wine

- Cheese and crackers.

- A dump bucket. Remember, you're tasting, not drinking. You can always go back and try the same one again at the end.

- Notepad to jot down observations.

See whether what you learned about the grape holds true on the palate, which example is "truer" than the others, and which characteristics are common throughout all the examples.

Blind Tasting

Each friend brings a bottle of a straightforward example of a grape. Each bottle is opened and bagged in a paper bag or covered in aluminum foil (be careful when holding the covered bottles, as they could easily slip out of your hand). Number the covered bottles. You can either list the grapes and, by tasting, determine which bottle is which or go "double blind" and not disclose any of the options at all. You'll need the following:

so you want to throw a wine party

- Wineglasses (one per person should be fine).

- Wine. Each friend brings a bottle of a straightforward example of a varietal. No blends or esoteric varietals, please!

- Paper bags or aluminum foil to wrap all the bottles.

- Marker to number each bottle.

- Use your tasting skills to make educated guesses about each wine. The friend with the most correct (or closest) guesses gets to pick which wine to take home.

- Notepads (given how analytical this tasting is, it's easier to write down your findings first, then guess which wine is which). As you taste over and over, your opinions may change. Keeping a running log helps remember your first gut reactions, which end up being correct more often than not.

This is a great way to hone your tasting skills. Remember to have fun, too!

wine

Vertical Tasting

If you're fortunate enough to have the same exact wine but from multiple years, then you *must* open them all at the same time and see how the wine changed from year to year. Observing the effects each vintage has on the wine and how the wine ages from year to year is a rare opportunity not to pass up. You'll need the following:

- Information on each vintage, if possible. Assuming the wine is consistent, knowing some of the intricacies from each year (e.g., by consulting vintage charts) can really help you understand how the different climatic influences from year to year affect the wine.

- Wine. Although it's possible to do this with only two wines, three wines (same wine from different years) really is the best place to start, especially if the years are consecutive. The more years, the better!

- Wineglasses, enough for each person to have each of the wines in a separate glass at the same time.

- Notepad.

- Cheese and crackers.

so you want to throw a wine party

Horizontal Tasting

As you can guess, this is the opposite of a vertical tasting. The goal is to taste a selection of wines from the same vintage. You'll need the following:

- Information on that specific vintage. Remember, the vintage is more the focus than the wine.

- Wine. Here are three ways to organize a horizontal tasting:
    - Different selections from the same winery from the same vintage, determining which selection was the winery's best effort that year.
    - Different wineries but same region, prices, vintage and varietal. By eliminating as many variables as you can, you really get a good look at how wineries and winemakers compare. A great example would be a yearly tasting of Beaujolais Nouveau.
    - Different wineries from different regions, but same price, vintage and varietal. Which region's 2007 Cabernet was best for the money? Do you prefer southern hemisphere Sauvignon Blancs to their northern hemisphere counterparts? These tastings really highlight how different regions produce different styles of wine.

- Wine glasses, enough for each person to have each wine in a separate glass in front of them.

- Notepad.

- Cheese and crackers.

Large-Format Tasting

It's not a big deal when a handful of people try wine from the same bottle, but it's extra special when twenty-five people get to try from one big bottle. You'll need the following:

- One big bottle of wine—the bigger the better. A regular 750-milliliter bottle provides ten 2.5-ounce pours (about half a glass). A magnum is twice as big (1.5 liters), and a jeroboam is twice as big as that (3 liters). Remember, not many people will make the trek to your place for a party where they drink only half a glass of wine. Make sure you have more wine to supplement or enough wine from the large bottle to satisfy your guests.

- Information about that specific wine.

- One wineglass per person.

- Cheese and crackers, as always. The notepad probably won't be necessary this time.

SO YOU WANT TO THROW A WINE PARTY

Characteristic Tasting

In this tasting the main focus is a certain flavor (raspberries, for example). You'll need the following:

- Examples of the flavor in question. If you're choosing cherries, then you should have red, black, Rainier, bing, and even Maraschino cherries on hand to eat. Other extensions such as cherry pie or cherry-flavored candy also would work.

- A few different bottles of wine that exhibit a strong example of the selected flavor. Watch as everyone learns to pinpoint exactly what type of cherries they're finding in the wine, just like the pros!

- Cheese and crackers. With this many flavors around, neutral-flavored food is more important than ever.

- Notepad to describe the differences. Try to apply the same terms you would with wine. Sweeter? More tart? More bitter?

wine

The Sub-$10 Faceoff

Make no mistake: This blind tasting is as competitive as it gets. Your reputation as a savvy wine shopper is on the line. You'll need the following:

- Wine. Everyone brings what they think is the best bottle of wine under $10. Price tags must still be attached or other proof provided on demand.

- One wineglass per person.

- Paper bags or aluminum foil to wrap bottles (hold on tight!).

- Marker to number wrapped bottles.

- Ranking sheet for guests to vote on. All sheets are collected and tallied.

- A couple of bucks from each guest to throw in the pot. The winner with the most votes gets to keep the pot.

so you want to throw a wine party

The Opening of a VSB (Very Special Bottle)

No plans for a Saturday night? Maybe it's time to open the VSB you've been sitting on for years. You'll need the following:

- Friends to cook and host. Hey, it's your VSB! Cooking dinner for you is a small price to pay.

- Wine—including your VSB, of course! Be sure to take care of all preparations, including decanting and temperature. You also want a reception wine (an easy-drinking wine to start the evening), a backup wine (just in case your VSB is off, heaven forbid!), and a dessert wine if your host is going all out.

- The full history of the VSB, including how you got it, why you still have it, and whether you've tried anything similar.

- Whatever happens, do not leave the party until someone else has committed to opening a VSB of their own the next time.

notes

COLLECT ALL TITLES IN THE POCKET POSH® SERIES!

Complete Calorie Counter

Word Power: 120 Words You Should Know

Word Power: 120 Words to Make You Sound Intelligent

Word Power: 120 Job Interview Words You Should Know

Word Power: 120 Words That Are Fun to Say

Dining Out Calorie Counter

Cocktails

Tips for Quilters

Tips for Knitters

First Aid

Guide to Great Home Video

Tips for Travelers

Wine

Tips for Bridge Players

Tips for Poker Players

Puzzle Series